Green Mona's Rhyming Reference

A book of word-endings, and associated rhymes, that can be looked up by sound. Easy to find rhymes based on sound.

Presented By:
Kaseyemm

Green Mona's Rhyming Reference

Kaseyemm

Wyoming Valley, Pennsylvania

Dedicated to all writers

Green Mona's Rhyming Reference

Forward

This reference book was put together for poets and songwriters, and anyone else that needs to rhyme. It is designed to assist in the creative process.

Thank you.
Kaseyemm

TABLE OF CONTENTS

	Page #
A	5
D	25
E	25
I	47
L	63
O	63
S	83
T	85
U	86
X	97

KASEYEMM

Wyoming Valley, Pennsylvania

"GREEN MONA'S RHYMING REFERENCE"

RHYME BY SOUND (look up by sound)

A

A (AYE)
away array bray betray blue-jay bouquet clay day decay delay disarray dismay display essay expose' fray gay gray hallway hay hey holiday hooray Jose' Kay lay matinee may naysay negligee obey pay play portray protégé ray resume' ricochet risqué rose' say slay sleigh soufflé stay stray sway they toupee' weigh way x-ray

A
Americana banana bandanna cabana Indiana nirvana

AB
blab cab crab dab drab gab grab jab lab nab scab slab stab tab

ABBLE
babble dabble rabble scrabble

ABLE
angel apple babble bubble cable chapel disable dabble dapple enable fable gamble

grapple grumble label Mabel muzzle particle
rabble ramble rumble scrabble scramble
scrapple sell shamble shovel stable table
unable unstable
also see : "angle"

ACE
base bass brace case chase commonplace
debase disgrace displace embrace encase
erase face grace lace mace misplace pace
place race replace space trace unlace vase

ACH (ATCH)
attach batch catch detach dispatch hatch latch
match patch scratch snatch

ACK
almanac attack black cardiac egomaniac
feedback hack haystack jack kleptomaniac
knack lack maniac pack plaque quack rack
sack shack slack snack stack tack track whack
Zodiac

ACKER
attacker backer blacker cracker hacker
nutcracker packer ransacker slacker smacker
tacker tracker

ACAL
empirical comfortable comical logical lyrical
miracle natural satirical
also see : "el", "ell", "l"

ACT
abstract attract backed compact contract
distract exact fact impact jacked packed pact
protract quack racked react sacked slacked
smacked snacked subtract tact tract whacked

ACTOR
actor benefactor contractor detractor distracter
extractor factor reactor refractor tractor
also see : "er"

AD
ad add brad cad chad clad dad egad fad glad
grad had lad mad nad nomad pad plaid rad
sad shad Trinidad

ADE (AID)
aid afraid arcade barricade blade blockade
braid brayed brigade centigrade charade
crusade degrade dismayed dissuade
downgrade escapade evade fade Gatorade
grade grenade hayed invade laid lemonade
made maid masquerade paid parade persuade
played promenade raid renegade serenade
shade spade stockade suede tirade trade

ADDLE
paddle, saddle straddle
also see : "attle"

AFE
waif

AFF (APH)

calf carafe epitaph giraffe graph paragraph phonograph photograph polygraph riffraff staff telegraph

AFFLE
baffle raffle snaffle
also see : "l", "ale"

AFT
craft draft graft overdraft witchcraft

AG
bag brag drag fag flag gag hag jag lag mag nag rag sag shag slag snag tag swag tag wag zag

AGE (long A)
age cage gage gauge page rage rampage sage stage wage

AGE
baggage carnage carriage disparage garbage marriage miscarriage wattage
also see : "edge"

AGE
barrage camouflage garage entourage mirage

AGER
lager

AGGER
bagger dagger stagger swagger

AID (ADE)

aid afraid arcade barricade blade blockade
braid brayed brigade centigrade charade
crusade degrade dismayed dissuade
downgrade escapade evade fade Gatorade
grade grenade hayed invade laid lemonade
made maid masquerade paid parade persuade
played promenade raid renegade serenade
shade spade stockade suede tirade trade

AIM (AME)
acclaim became blame came claim exclaim
fame flame frame game inflame lame maim
name proclaim same shame tame

AIN (ANE)
abstain again airplane arraign ascertain attain
brain campaign cane chain champagne
cocaine complain contain crane detain disdain
domain drain entertain explain feign gain grain
humane hurricane hydroplane insane lane
main maintain mane migraine obtain ordain
pain pane pertain plain plane profane propane
rain refrain reign rein remain sane slain Spain
sprain stain strain sustain train vain vane vein
wane
also see : "ang"

AINT
acquaint ain't complaint faint paint quaint
restraint saint taint

AIR
air affair anywhere aware bare bear billionaire
blare care chair compare dare debonair
declare despair disrepair elsewhere

everywhere fair fare flair glare hair hare heir
impair mare millionaire nightmare pair pare
pear prayer prepare rare repair scare snare
solitaire somewhere spare square stair stare
swear tear their thoroughfare unaware
underwear unfair ware wear where
also see : "ear", "er"

AIRY (EARY) (ERRY)
adversary airy arbitrary beneficiary berry bury
canary capillary cautionary cherry commentary
culinary customary dairy dictionary dietary
dignitary disciplinary discretionary evolutionary
extraordinary fairy ferry hairy hereditary
honorary imaginary intermediary legendary
mercenary military momentary monetary
mortuary nary necessary obituary ordinary
planetary prairie pulmonary reactionary
revolutionary sanctuary sanitary scary
secretary seminary sherry solitary stationary
temporary very visionary vocabulary voluntary
wary

AISLE (ILE)
aisle awhile bile compile crocodile defile file
isle juvenile meanwhile mile Nile pile rile smile
style tile trial vile while worthwhile zile

AJOR
cager major pager stager wager

AKE
ache bake brake break cake fake flake forsake
headache heartache keepsake lake make

mistake opaque quake rake shake snake stake steak take wake

AKER
acre baker breaker faker maker pacemaker peacemaker Quaker shaker strikebreaker taker troublemaker undertaker watchmaker

AKLE
cackle crackle hackle shackle tackle

AL
canal chorale gal morale pal shall

ALD
appalled bald balled called scald stalled
also : Add "ed" to "all" words

ALE
ale bail bale blackmail braille cocktail curtail exhale fail female frail hail hale impale inhale jail mail male nail pale prevail rail sail scale shale snail stale tail they'll veil whale

ALER
inhaler jailer sailor staler trailer wailer
see also : "er"

ALF
calf carafe epitaph giraffe graph laugh paragraph phonograph photography polygraph riffraff staff telegraph

ALID
ballad invalid salad valid

see also : "id"

ALL
all artificial ball beneficial brawl call crawl doll drawl enthrall fall gall haul initial install judicial mall maul nightfall official overhaul parasol pitfall protocol rainfall sacrificial scrawl shawl small snowfall snow-squall sprawl squall stall superficial tall thrall wall waterfall

ALLEY
alley bally dilly-dally galley rally tally valley

ALLOW
allow avow bough bow brow chow cow disavow endow frau how now plough plow row slough somehow sow thou vow wow

ALM (OMB)
aplomb bomb calm embalm mom palm psalm qualm

ALORIE
calorie gallery salary

ALT
assault cobalt exalt fault halt malt salt somersault vault

AM
am anagram arteriogram cam clam cram dam damn diaphragm gram ham jam lamb ma'am mammogram madam scram sham slam swam telegram tram yam

AMA (OMMA)
comma drama llama mama melodrama pajama

AMBLE
amble gamble ramble scramble shamble

AME (AIM)
acclaim became blame came claim exclaim
fame flame frame game inflame lame maim
name proclaim same shame tame

AMMA
Bahama comma dalai drama lama llama
melodrama pajama

AMMER
clamor glamour grammar hammer slammer
stammer yammer

AMP
amp camp champ clamp cramp damp lamp
ramp revamp stamp vamp

AMPLE
ample example sample trample
see also : "el"

AN
artesian ban can fan human Iran man pan
partisan plan ran tan
also see : "en"

ANCE (ENCE)
advance alliance appliance ants chance
circumstance compliance dance enhance

extragravance finance France glance lance
pants prance reliance romance stance trance

abstinence adolescence affluence alliance
appearance adherence assistance assurance
benevolence clearance coherence coincidence
commence competence compliance condense
conference confidence consequence
consistence convalescence convenience
defense defiance difference disappearance
dispense dissidence distance eloquence
endurance evidence excellence existence
expense experience immense importance
impotence incense incidence incoherence
incompetence indigence influence innocence
insistence insurance intense interference
intolerance magnificence negligence
obedience perseverance permanence
persistence preference pretense reference
reliance resistance sense suspense tense
tolerance violence

ANCH
avalanche branch ranch

AND
and band bland brand canned command
contraband demand expand fanned gland
grand grandstand hand handstand land
panned planned reprimand sand stand
understand

ANDLE
candle dandle handle sandal scandal vandal

ANDY
andy brandy dandy handy randy sandy

ANE (AIN)
abstain again airplane arraign ascertain attain
brain campaign cane chain champagne
cocaine complain contain crane detain disdain
domain drain entertain explain feign gain grain
humane hurricane hydroplane insane lane
main maintain mane migraine obtain ordain
pain pane pertain plain plane profane propane
rain refrain reign rein remain sane slain Spain
sprain stain strain sustain train vain vane vein
wane

ANNET
gannet granite Janet planet
also see : "et", "it"

ANG
bang boomerang clang dang fang rag sang
slang sprang
See also : "ain"

ANGE
arrange change derange estrange exchange
range strange

ANGLE
angle dangle entangle jangle mangle particle
spangle strangle tangle triangle wrangle
also see : "able"

ANK
bank blank clank dank drank flank frank hank plank prank rank sank shrank spank tank thank yank

ANNEL
channel flannel panel

ANNER
banner canner fanner manner manor planner scanner spanner tanner

ANNUAL
annual manual

ANT
ant aunt can't chant decant enchant grant implant pant plant rant scant shan't slant sub-plant transplant
also see : "ent"

ANY
Benny Jenny many penny

AP
cap chap clap flap gap handicap lap map mishap nap rap sap scrap slap snap strap tap trap wrap zap

APE
ape cape drape escape grape landscape rape seascape shape tape

APER
caper draper escaper paper raper scraper
shaper skyscraper taper
also see : " er"

APH (AFF)
calf carafe epitaph giraffe graph paragraph
phonograph photograph polygraph riffraff staff
telegraph

APS
caps collapse craps elapse flaps lapse maps
naps perhaps saps traps wraps
also add "s" to "ap" words

APE
ape cape crepe drape escape grape landscape
rape scrape seascape shape tape

APPY
crappie happy nappy pappy sappy scrappy
slaphappy yappy

ARB
barb carb garb

ARCH
arch march parch starch

ARD
bombard card chard discard disregard guard
hard lard regard retard tarred yard

ARE
are bar bazaar bizarre car caviar cigar disbar
far guitar jar par scar sitar spar star tar

ARF
barf scarf snarf

ARGE
barge charge discharge enlarge large

ARK
aardvark arc bark dark embark hark lark mark
narc nark park patriarch remark shark spark
stark

ARM
alarm arm charm disarm farm forearm harm

ARN
barn darn yarn

ARP
carp harp sharp

ARROW
arrow barrow harrow marrow narrow sparrow
tarot
also see : "owe"

ARSH
harsh marsh

ART
art apart cart chart counterpart dart depart fart heart mart part smart start sweetheart tart upstart

ARTED
brokenhearted carted charted darted departed fainthearted halfhearted smarted started

ARTER
barter carter charter darter garter martyr smarter starter tartar tarter

ARV
carve starve

AS (AZZ)
as has jazz whereas

ASH
ash balderdash bash brash cash clash crash dash flash gnash hash lash mash rash rehash slash smash stash thrash trash

ASK
ask bask cask flask mask masque task

ASP
clasp gasp grasp

ASS
amass ass bass brass crass gas glass grass harass hourglass lass mass morass mustache overpass pass sassafras surpass

AST
aghast blast cast classed contrast fast
flabbergast forecast gassed last mast outlast
overcast passed past vast

ASTE
aftertaste baste braced distaste faced haste
lambaste paste taste waist waste

ASTER
blaster caster castor disaster faster forecaster
master pastor plaster postmaster taskmaster

ASTIC
bombastic drastic elastic enthusiastic fantastic
gymnastic plastic sarcastic scholastic spastic

AT
acrobat aristocrat autocrat bat brat bureaucrat
cat chat democrat diplomat drat fat flat gnat hat
mat pat rat sat scat spat stat thermostat vat

ATCH (ACH)
attach batch catch detach dispatch hatch latch
match patch scratch snatch
also see : "etch"

ATE
Ate One syllable:
ate bait date eight fate hate late mate plate rate
skate slate state straight strait trait wait weight

Ate Two syllable:
await berate castrate debate dictate donate
equate estate frustrate irate locate narrate

ornate placate relate rotate sedate translate vacate

Ate Three syllable:
Abdicate advocate aggravate agitate amputate animate annotate arbitrate assimilate calculate candidate captivate celebrate circulate compensate complicate concentrate confiscate consecrate constipate consummate contemplate correlate culminate cultivate decimate decorate dedicate demonstrate desecrate designate detonate devastate dislocate dissipate dominate duplicate educate ejaculate elevate estimate excavate fabricate fascinate fluctuate formulate generate graduate gravitate heavyweight hesitate hibernate illustrate imitate implicate incubate innovate inordinate insulate isolate lacerate legislate levitate liberate liquidate lubricate magistrate marinate masturbate mediate moderate modulate motivate nominate operate orchestrate oscillate overate overstate overweight penetrate perpetrate populate punctuate radiate regulate reinstate renovate ruminate saturate separate simulate situate speculate stimulate stipulate suffocate tabulate terminate titillate tolerate underrate understate underweight vaccinate validate vegetate ventilate vindicate violate

Ate Four or more syllable:
accelerate accentuate accommodate accumulate affiliate alienate annihilate appreciate appropriate articulate assassinate associate collaborate commemorate

commiserate communicate conciliate
congratulate consolidate contaminate
cooperate coordinate corroborate decapitate
deliberate depreciate deteriorate discriminate
elaborate eliminate emancipate emulate
enunciate eradicate evacuate evaluate
evaporate excommunicate exonerate
extenuate exterminate facilitate humiliate
illuminate incapacitate incarcerate incorporate
infatuate impersonate insinuate intimidate
intoxicate invigorate manipulate necessitate
negotiate obliterate originate participate
precipitate procrastinate reciprocate regurgitate
reiterate rejuvenate resuscitate retaliate
subordinate

ATH
aftermath bath Cath math path psychopath
sociopath wrath

ATTLE
battle cattle embattle paddle rattle tattle
also see : "addle"

AUD (ODD)
abroad applaud awed broad clod cod defraud
façade fraud God nod odd pod prod
promenade quad rod shod sod squad trod wad

AUDY (ODDY)
embody bawdy body gaudy lawdy nobody
shoddy somebody toddy

AUGHT (OT) (OUGHT)

astronaut Bought brought caught cosmonaut
fought naught ought sought taught thought
wrought

AUNT
aunt daunt flaunt gaunt haunt flaunt jaunt taunt
want

AV
calve have lav savv

AVAGE
lavage ravage savage scavage

AVE
behave brave cave concave crave engrave
forgave gave grave knave pave rave save
shave slave waive wave

AVEL
gavel gravel ravel travel unravel

AVER
braver cadaver favor flavor graver paver saver
savor shaver waiver waver

AW
awe bra caw claw flaw gnaw jaw law ma
overdraw paw raw saw slaw squaw straw thaw
withdraw

AWN (ON)
Amazon autobahn bonbon Bonn brawn chiffon
dawn drawn echelon fawn gone lawn neon on

pawn pentagon silicon swan undergone upon
wan yawn

AWS (OZ)
applause because cause Claus clause claws
gauze gnaws jaws laws menopause Oz pause
paws straws vas was
also : add "s" to "aw" words

AX
ax backs blacks fax jacks lax max relax packs
sax slacks tax wax

AYE (A)
away array bay bray betray blue-jay bouquet
clay day decay delay disarray dismay display
essay expose' fray gay gray hallway hay hey
holiday hooray Jose' Kay lay matinee may
naysay negligee obey pay play portray protégé
ray resume' ricochet risqué rose' say slay
sleigh soufflé stay stray sway they toupee'
weigh way x-ray

AYER
betrayer conveyor grayer layer mayor payor
player portrayer prayer slayer soothsayer
sprayer stayer surveyor

AZE
ablaze always appraise bays betrays blaze
bouquets braze craze days daze decays
delays disarrays displays faze gaze glaze
graze hallways haze lays malaise mayonnaise
maze nays nowadays obeys pays phase

phrase plays polonaise portrays praise rays
raze slays stays sways ways weighs

AZER
appraiser blazer gazer laser maser phaser
praiser razor

AZEY
crazy daisy hazy lazy

D

DONE (UN)
anyone begun bun comparison denizen engine
everyone fun gun hyperion jettison none nun
oblivion one outdone outrun overdone overrun
phenomenon pun puritan run shun simpleton
skeleton son stun sun ton undone unison
venison

E

E (long E)
E one syllable:
be bee fee flea flee free gee glee he key knee
me plea pea pee sea see she tea thee tree we

E two syllable:
agree baby belly cherry debris decree degree
deli flighty foresee goatee hee-hee maybe
many penny plenty rightly smelly theory trustee
wintry

E three syllable:

absentee agency agony almighty amnesty
ancestry archery armory artistry bakery
balcony battery bigotry blasphemy botany
bourgeoisie bravery brevity bribery burglary
casualty cavalry cavity century certainty charity
chastity chickadee chimpanzee chivalry
clemency colony comedy company courtesy
crudity cruelty cursory custody decency deputy
destiny diary dignity disagree drapery dynasty
ebony ecstasy effigy elegy embassy employee
enemy energy eulogy factory fallacy family
fantasy felony fertility fiery flagrancy flattery
fluency forgery frequency galaxy gallantry
gallery gravity guarantee harmony heresy
hierarchy history homily honesty imagery
industry infamy infancy infantry injury inquiry
irony ivory jamboree jealousy jeopardy jewelry
jubilee legacy leniency levity liberty liturgy
lottery loyalty lunacy luxury melody memory
mercury mimicry ministry misery mockery
modesty mutiny mystery nominee nursery
odyssey oversee pageantry papacy parody
paternity pedigree penalty perjury piracy
pleasantry poetry poignancy policy potpourri
poverty privacy prodigy property puberty purity
quality quantity rarity recipe rectory referee
refugee remedy repartee revelry rhapsody
rivalry robbery rosemary royalty salary sanctity
sanity savory scarcity scenery scrutiny secrecy
sesame shivery simile slavery slippery sorcery
strategy subsidy subtlety sugary summary
symmetry sympathy symphony tapestry
tendency thievery timpani treachery trilogy
trinity truancy tyranny unity urgency victory
watery witchery

E four or more syllable:
ability absurdity activity actuality adversity
affinity agility ambiguity amenity animosity
anarchy anatomy anniversary anonymity
antiquity anxiety Aphrodite artillery astrology
astronomy atrocity audacity authenticity
authority barbarity biography biology brilliancy
brutality capacity captivity celebrity Christianity
chronology commodity community compatibility
complacency complexity complimentary
comprehensibility conformity consistency
conspiracy contradictory criminality curiosity
debauchery deformity delivery dependency
depravity diversity diplomacy directory discover
discrepancy divinity eccentricity economy
efficiency electricity elementary emergency
enormity epitome equality eternity expectancy
extremity facility facsimile ferocity fertility
festivity fidelity formality fraternity futility
generosity geography geometry gratuity
heredity hospitality hostility humanity humility
hypocrisy identity idiocy illiteracy immodesty
immunity impropriety inability incapacity
inconsistency indecency independently
individuality inferiority infirmary ingenuity
inhumanity insufficiency insurgency integrity
intensity legality liberty longevity machinery
mahogany majesty maternity maturity
mediocrity mightily minority mobility monogamy
monopoly monstrosity morality mythology
nationality nativity necessity neutrality nobility
notoriety objectively peculiarity personality
philanthropy philosophy photography popularity
pornography posterity profanity proficiency

promiscuity propriety prosperity priority
proximity psychiatry publicity reality recovery
rudimentary satisfactory security sensibility
sensuality serenity severity sexuality similarity
simplicity sincerity sobriety society sophistry
spontaneity stability sterility stupidity
subjectively superficially superiority technicality
theology totality tranquility triviality uniformity
university utility validity variety velocity virginity
vulgarity

EACH
beach breach each impeach leech peach
preach reach screech speech teach

EACHER
bleacher creature feature preacher teacher

EAD (EED)
agreed bleed breed centipede concede creed
deed exceed feed greed inbreed knead lead
mislead need precede proceed read recede
reed secede seed speed stampede succeed
tweed weed

EAF (EEF)
beef belief brief chief disbelief grief leaf reef
relief thief

EAGER
beleaguer eager intriguer leaguer meager
overeager

EAG
fatigue intrigue league

EAGLE
beagle eagle illegal legal regal seagull

EAK (EEK)
beak bleak creak eek freak leak meek reek
seek speak tweak weak week

EAL (EEL)
appeal automobile conceal deal eel feel
genteel he'll heal heel ideal kneel meal mobile
peel real reel repeal reveal seal she'll spiel
squeal steel steal veal we'll wheal zeal

EALED (EELED) (EILD)
battlefield field shield wield yield

EALER
congealer dealer feeler healer sealer squealer
stealer wheeler

EALTH
health stealth wealth

EAM
beam cream deem dream esteem extreme
gleam ream regime scheme scream seam
seen steam stream supreme team teem

EAN (EEN)
bean between caffeine canteen chlorine clean
codeine convene cuisine dean demean
evergreen foreseen gasoline green guillotine
Halloween in-between intervene kerosene lean
lien machine marine mean mezzanine

nectarine nicotine obscene preen quarantine
queen ravine routine sardine scene seen
serene spleen submarine tambourine tangerine
teen thirteen fourteen fifteen sixteen seventeen
eighteen nineteen Vaseline wolverine
see also : "in"

EAP (EEP)
barkeep beep cheap cheep deep heap keep
leap peep reap seep sheep sleep steep sweep
weep

EAR
adhere appear atmosphere auctioneer beer
bombardier career cashier cavalier chandelier
cheer clear dear deer disappear ear engineer
fear frontier gear hear hemisphere here
insincere interfere jeer leer mere mountaineer
overhear peer persevere pioneer queer
racketeer reappear rear revere seer severe
shear sheer sincere smear sneer spear sphere
steer stratosphere tear veneer volunteer where
year
also see : "er", "air"

EARD
appeared beard cleared disappeared feared
jeered persevered smeared speared weird

EARL
curl earl girl hurl pearl swirl twirl whirl

EARN (URN)
adjourn burn churn concern discern earn fern intern kern learn overturn return sojourn spurn stern taciturn turn urn yearn

EARNY (OURNEY)
attorney journey tourney

EARSE (URSE)
adverse converse curse disburse disperse diverse hearse immerse inverse nurse purse rehearse reverse terse transverse traverse universe verse worse

EARTH
birth dearth earth girth mirth worth

EARY (AIRY) (ERRY)
adversary airy arbitrary beneficiary berry Bury canary capillary cautionary cherry commentary culinary customary dairy dictionary dietary dignitary disciplinary discretionary evolutionary extraordinary fairy ferry hairy hereditary honorary imaginary intermediary legendary mercenary military momentary monetary mortuary nary necessary obituary ordinary planetary prairie pulmonary reactionary revolutionary sanctuary sanitary scary secretary seminary sherry solitary stationary temporary very visionary vocabulary voluntary wary

EASE (EEZ) (EAZ)
aborigines appease bees breeze cheese disease ease expertise freeze keys knees

peas pleas please sees seize sleaze squeeze
tease trapeze

EASE
cease crease decease fleece geese grease
increase lease mantelpiece masterpiece peace
piece police release

EASON
reason season
also see : "un"

EAST
beast ceased creased deceased east feast
least pieced priest yeast

EAT
athlete beat beet bittersweet bleat cheat
compete complete conceit concrete deceit
defeat delete deplete discreet discrete eat elite
feat feet fleet greet heat incomplete indiscreet
meat meet mistreat neat obsolete parakeet
receipt repeat retreat seat sheet sleet street
suite sweet treat wheat

EATH
beneath heath teeth underneath wreath

EATHER
altogether feather leather tether together
weather whether
also see : "er"

EAVE
achieve believe bereave conceive disbelieve
eve grieve heave leave perceive receive
relieve reprieve retrieve sleeve Steve weave

EAZ (EEZ) (EASE)
aborigines appease bees breeze cheese
disease ease expertise freeze keys knees
peas pleas please sees seize sleaze squeeze
tease trapeze

ECK
check deck fleck heck neck peck Quebec
speck trek wreck

ECKS (X) (EX)
complex decks duplex ex flex necks pecks
reflex rolodex sex specs unisex

ECT
affect architect bisect checked collect connect
correct defect deflect derelict dialect direct
disinfect dissect effect eject erect expect
incorrect inject neglect object pecked perfect
project prospect protect recollect reflect reject
respect select subject suspect wrecked
also see : "act", "ept", "ict"

ECTER
collector connector detector deflector director
injector inspector nectar objector projector
prospector reflector selector vector
also see : "er"

ED
ahead bed bedspread bread bred coed dead
dread fed figurehead fled flowerbed head
inbred lead led misled misread read red said
shed shred sled spread thread wed

EDDLE
medal meddle metal pedal peddle

EDGE
allege dredge edge fledge hedge ledge
privilege sacrilege sledge wedge
see also : "age"

EED (EAD)
agreed bleed breed centipede concede creed
deed exceed feed greed inbreed knead lead
mislead need precede proceed read recede
reed secede seed speed stampede succeed
tweed weed

EEF (EAF)
beef belief brief chief disbelief grief leaf reef
relief thief

EEING
agreeing being decreeing disagreeing
farseeing fleeing foreseeing freeing
guaranteeing overseeing seeing

EEK (EAK)
beak bleak creak eek freak leak meek reek
seek speak tweak weak week

EEL (EAL)

appeal automobile conceal deal eel feel
genteel he'll heal heel ideal kneel meal mobile
peel real reel repeal reveal seal she'll spiel
squeal steel steal veal we'll wheal zeal

EELD (EALED) (IELD)
battlefield field shield wield yield

EEN (EAN)
bean between caffeine canteen chlorine clean
codeine convene cuisine dean demean
evergreen foreseen gasoline green guillotine
Halloween in-between intervene kerosene lean
lien machine marine mean mezzanine
nectarine nicotine obscene preen quarantine
queen ravine routine sardine scene seen
serene spleen submarine tambourine tangerine
teen thirteen fourteen fifteen sixteen seventeen
eighteen nineteen Vaseline wolverine
see also : "in"

EEP (EAP)
barkeep beep cheap cheep deep heap keep
leap peep reap seep sheep sleep steep sweep
weep

EEVE
achieve believe bereave conceive disbelieve
eve grieve heave leave perceive receive
relieve reprieve retrieve sleeve Steve weave

EEZ (EAZ) (EASE)
aborigines appease bees breeze cheese
disease ease expertise freeze keys knees

peas pleas please sees seize sleaze squeeze tease trapeze

EF
chef clef deaf

EFT
cleft deft left theft

EEGAL (EAGLE)
beagle eagle illegal legal regal seagull

EEVER
achiever beaver believer cleaver deceiver fever leaver receiver reliever retriever weaver

EGG
beg egg keg leg peg

IELED (EALED) (EELED)
battlefield field shield wield yield

EKKO
echo deco gecko
also see : "owe"

EL
apparel artificial barrel beneficial cattle chattel carol confidential credential differential embattle essential influential initial judicial nonessential official potential preferential presidential prudential rattle residential sacrificial sequential superficial tattle torrential
also see : "ell"

ELCH
belch squelch welch

ELD
deld felled gelled held meld upheld weld

ELF
elf herself himself itself myself shelf yourself

ELL
bell belle caramel carrousel cell clientele dell
dwell excel farewell fell gel hell hotel infidel
knell mademoiselle personnel sell shell smell
tell well yell
also see : "el"

ELLER
cellar dweller feller propeller seller smeller
speller stellar sweller teller
also see : "er"

ELLO
bellow cello fellow hello yellow

ELM
elm helm realm overwhelm whelm

ELP
help kelp yelp

ELT
belt Celt dealt felt heartfelt melt pelt welt

ELVE
delve shelve twelve

EM
Bethlehem condemn gem hem requiem stem them

EMBER
December dismember ember member November remember September
Also see : "er"

EMPT
attempt contempt dreamt exempt tempt

EN
amen citizen den fen hen hydrogen men oxygen pen regimen specimen ten then yen Zen

EN (N)
achin' amen bacon beaten cheatin' citizen den eaten fakin' fen forsaken hen hydrogen Jamaican makin' men mistaken overtaken oxygen pen regimen shaken specimen sweeten taken ten then unbeaten women yen Zen
also see : "an"

ENCH
bench clench drench French quench stench trench wench wrench

END
apprehend attend ascend attend befriend bend blend commend comprehend condescend defend depend descend dividend end expend

extend fend friend intend lend mend offend
penned pretend recommend send spend tend
transcend trend unbend

ENDENT
ascendant attendant defendant dependent
descendant independent pendant
superintendent transcendent

ENDER
bender blender contender defender extender
fender gender lender mender offender
pretender sender slender spender splendor
surrender suspender vendor weekender
also see : " enter"

ENGE
avenge revenge

ENSE (ANCE)
abstinence affluence alliance appearance
adherence assistance assurance benevolence
clearance coherence coincidence commence
competence compliance condense conference
confidence consequence consistence
convenience defense defiance difference
disappearance dispense dissidence distance
eloquence endurance evidence excellence
existence expense experience fence immense
importance impotence incense incidence
incoherence incompetence indigence influence
innocence insistence insurance intense
interference intolerance magnificence
negligence obedience perseverance
permanence persistence preference pretense

reference reliance resistance sense suspense tense tolerance violence

ENSED
against condensed fenced sensed

ENT
abandonment absent accent accident acknowledgment advertisement affluent ailment argument armament assent assistant attendant augment banishment basement benevolent bent cement cent circumvent coincident comment competent compliment condiment confident continent convent consent consistent content curtailment defendant descent descendant dent detriment development distant document elegant element embarrassment embellishment embezzlement embodiment eminent encouragement enlightenment environment establishment event existent experiment ferment fluent frequent gent government impalement implement imprisonment incident incompetent inconsistent indent independent ingredient insistent intelligent intent invent lent Lent management meant measurement merriment misrepresent monument nourishment orient ornament parliament pendant percent permanent persistent precedent predicament present president prevent prominent punishment regiment relent rent repent replenishment represent resent resident resistant reverent sacrament sediment sent sentiment settlement spent subsequent succulent superintendent supplement

temperament tenement tent testament torment
tournament transcendent unbent vent violent
went wonderment
also see : "ant"

ENTAL
accidental coincidental continental dental
departmental detrimental experimental
fundamental gentle governmental incidental
identical intercontinental lentil mental
monumental oriental parental regimental rental
rudimental sentimental supplemental
temperamental
also see : "el"

ENTER
center dissenter enter experimenter frequenter
inventor mentor presenter preventer renter
tormentor
also see : "ender"

ENTITY
amenity identity obscenity serenity
also see : "e"

EPT
accept adept crept except intercept kept
overslept slept stepped swept wept

ER
adventure after altar amateur anchor banker
better blur canker chauffeur concur confer
debtor defaulter defer denture deter falter
flanker franker fur grafter halter incur indenture
infer laughter letter misadventure occur per

prefer purr rafter ranker recur sir slur spanker
spur stir sweater tanker thereafter transfer
venture were wetter
also see : "ear", "air", "ure"

ERD (URD)(IRD)
absurd bird curd herd heard third word

ERGE (URGE)
converge dirge diverge emerge merge purge
sourge serge splurge submerge surge urge
verge

ERK (IRK)
clerk irk jerk lurk murk perk quirk shirk smirk
work

ERM (IRM)
affirm confirm firm germ reaffirm sperm squirm
term worm

ERNEL (OURNAL)
colonel eternal external fraternal infernal
journal kernel maternal nocturnal paternal

ERNT (URNT)
burnt weren't

ERROR
bearer carer darer error terror wearer
also see : "er"

ERRY (EARY) (AIRY)
adversary airy arbitrary beneficiary berry bury
canary capillary cautionary cherry commentary

culinary customary dairy dictionary dietary dignitary disciplinary discretionary evolutionary extraordinary fairy ferry hairy hereditary honorary imaginary intermediary legendary mercenary military momentary monetary mortuary nary necessary obituary ordinary planetary prairie pulmonary reactionary revolutionary sanctuary sanitary scary secretary seminary sherry solitary stationary temporary very visionary vocabulary voluntary wary

ERST (URST)
burst cursed first nursed outburst worst

ERT (URT) (IRT)
alert avert blurt comfort concert convert curt desert dessert dirt divert exert expert extrovert flirt hurt insert introvert invert pervert shirt skirt squirt subvert yogurt

ERVE
conserve curve deserve nerve observe preserve reserve serve swerve

ESK
burlesque desk grotesque picturesque

ESS
access address assess bashfulness bitterness bless caress chess cleverness cloudiness compress craziness deadliness depress digress distress dizziness dress duress eagerness easiness eeriness excess express finesse foolishness ghostliness guess

happiness haziness homelessness
hopelessness impress joyfulness laziness less
limitless mess nervousness obsess openness
oppress outrageousness penniless playfulness
possess press profess progress recess regress
repossess repress SOS steadiness
spaciousness stress success suppress
thoughtfulness transgress usefulness
viciousness willingness yes

EST
arrest attest best blessed breast Celeste chest
congest contest crest detest digest divest
dressed guessed guest infest ingest interest
invest jest manifest messed molest nest pest
protest request rest suggest test unrest vest
zest

ESTER
Chester contester fester investor jester Lester
molester pester protester semester sequester
tester Westchester Winchester

ET
alphabet basket bayonet bet blanket bracket
brunette cabinet cadet casket cigarette clarinet
comet cornet corvette debt docket duet epithet
etiquette faggot forget fret gasket gazette
jacket jet it let locket met net omelet packet pet
pocket quartet racket regret rocket roulette set
silhouette socket sprocket sunset sweat threat
toilet upset vet violet wet yet
also see : "it"

ETAL (ETTLE)
kettle mettle metal petal resettle settle
also see : "eddle"

ETCH
catch etch fetch retch sketch stretch wretch
also see : "atch"

ETH
breath death meth

ETHER
altogether feather leather tether together
weather whether
also see : "er"

ETTER
better debtor getter letter setter sweater wetter

ETTI
confetti jetty machete petty spaghetti sweaty

EATTLE (ETAL)
kettle mettle metal petal resettle settle
also see : "eddle"

EVE
achieve believe bereave conceive disbelieve
eve grieve heave leave perceive receive
relieve reprieve retrieve sleeve Steve weave

EVEL
bedevil bevel devil dishevel level revel

EVER
clever endeavor ever forever however lever never sever whatever whenever wherever whoever

EW (OO) (U)
accrue adieu ado anew avenue bamboo barbecue bayou blew blue boo brew caribou cashew chew choo-choo clue construe coo coup crew cue curfew debut dew drew due ensue ewe few flew flue glue grew guru honeydew igloo impromptu interview into issue Jew kangaroo kazoo lieu misconstrue moo new outdo overdue pew preview pursue rendezvous renew residue revenue review screw shampoo shoe shrew slew slue spew stew subdue sue taboo tattoo threw through tissue to too true two undo undue view voodoo withdrew you zoo

EWEL (UEL)
cruel duel fuel jewel

EWER
bluer brewer doer fewer interviewer newer reviewer sewer skewer viewer wooer

EYE (I)
alibi amplify barfly butterfly buy by bye certify clarify crucify defy deny die dignify diversify dry dye eye firefly fly fry glorify gratify guy high hi horrify I identify imply July justify lie lullaby modify my mystify notify passerby petrify pie pry qualify rely rye satisfy shy sigh signify

simplify sky sly solidify specify spry spy terrify
testify thigh tie try underlie verify why

EX (ECKS) (X)
complex decks duplex ex flex necks pecks
reflex rolodex sex specs unisex

EXT
context flexed next pretext text

EYES (IZE)

EZY
breezy cheesy easy queasy sleazy sneezy
speakeasy wheezy

I

I (EYE)
alibi amplify barfly butterfly buy by bye certify
clarify crucify defy deny die dignify diversify dry
dye eye firefly fly fry glorify gratify guy high hi
horrify I identify imply July justify lie lullaby
modify my mystify notify passerby petrify pie
pry qualify rely rye satisfy shy sigh signify
simplify sky sly solidify specify spry spy terrify
testify thigh tie try underlie verify why

IAL
cereal denial dial immaterial material
managerial ministerial retrial trial viol
also see : "ile"

IANT
client compliant defiant giant reliant

IB
adlib crib fib glib rib

IBE
bribe circumscribe describe jibe prescribe
scribe subscribe tribe

IBBLE
dribble kibble nibble quibble scribble sibyl

ICE
advice concise devise dice entice ice lice mice
nice paradise precise price rice sacrifice spice
splice suffice thrice twice vice

ICED
Christ diced feist heist iced

ICH (ITCH)
bewitch bitch ditch enrich glitch hitch pitch rich
snitch stitch switch twitch which

ICK
academic acrobatic aesthetic alphabetic
angelic analytic anatomic apathetic apologetic
aristocratic arithmetic aromatic arsenic arthritic
atomic attic autocratic brick bureaucratic
Catholic chromatic cinematic click climatic
comic cosmetic democratic dick dogmatic
dramatic economic endemic energetic
epidemic erratic fanatic flick genetic hick
hypocritic kick lick limerick lunatic magic
maverick melodramatic nick pathetic pick
poetic polemic pragmatic prick problematic

relic Semitic sick slick static stick sympathetic
synthetic systematic thematic thick tick
traumatic wick
also see : "ict"

ICKEN
chicken quicken sicken stricken thicken
also see : "in"

ICKET
cricket picket thicket ticket wicket
also see : "et", "it"

ICKS (IKS)
acrobatics bics crucifix fiddlesticks kicks licks
mathematics mix nix pix picks politics six sticks
ticks transfix tricks wicks

ICKSER (IXXER)
elixir fixer fixture mixer mixture

ICLE
bicycle icicle tricycle

ICT
addict conflict constrict contradict convict
derelict evict inflict licked predict pricked strict
also see : "ick"

ICTION
addiction affliction benediction contradiction
conviction crucifixion depiction diction eviction
fiction friction jurisdiction prediction restriction

ID
ballad bid did forbid grid hid invalid kid lid
pyramid rid salad skid slid squid valid

IDE
beside bonafide bride collide confide
countryside decide defied died dignified dived
eyed guide hide hillside homicide inside lied
outside pride provide reside ride side slide
snide stride subdivide subside suicide tide tried
wide yuletide

IDER
chider cider decider divider glider insider
outsider provider rider slider spider wider
see also : "er"

IDGE
bridge fridge ridge

IDDLE
diddle fiddle griddle middle riddle twiddle

IELD (EALED) (EELED)
battlefield field shield wield yield

IEN (IAN)
alien Australian

IER
barrier carrier terrier
also see : "er"

IET
diet riot quiet

IFE
knife life strife wife

IFF
cliff handkerchief if sniff stiff tiff whiff

IFLE
Eiffel eyeful rifle stifle trifle

IFT
drift gift lift shift swift thrift

IG
big dig fig gig jig pig rig swig twig wig

IGGET
digit midget fidget widget
also see : "et", "it"

IGID
frigid rigid

IGGLE
giggle jiggle squiggle wiggle wriggle

IKE
bike like mike spike strike tyke

IKER
biker hiker piker spiker spikier striker

IKS (ICKS)

acrobatics bics crucifix fiddlesticks kicks licks
mathematics mix nix pix picks politics six sticks
ticks transfix tricks wicks

ILD
child dialed mild piled smiled wild

ILE (AISLE)
aisle awhile bile compile crocodile defile file
isle juvenile meanwhile mile Nile pile rile smile
style tile trial vile while worthwhile zile

ILK
bilk ilk milk silk

ILL
bill chill daffodil distill drill fill frill fulfill gill grill hill
ill instill kill mill nil quill shrill sill skill spill still
swill thrill till trill until will windmill windowsill

ILLER
caterpillar chiller distiller driller filler instiller
killer pillar shriller spiller swiller thriller tiller

ILLED
billed build chilled drilled filled guild killed
rebuild willed
also add "ed" to "ill" above

ILLING
billing chilling distilling drilling filling fulfilling
instilling killing milling shrilling spilling stilling
swilling thrilling tilling unwilling

ILLION
billion Brazilian million Maximillian pavilion
reptilian trillion zillion

ILLOW
armadillo billow peccadillo pillow willow

ILT (UILT)
built guilt hilt jilt kilt quilt spilt stilt tilt wilt

IM
brim dim gym grim him limb pseudonym skim
slim swim trim whim

IME
climb crime dime I'm lime prime rhyme slime
summertime thyme time

IMMER
dimmer glimmer grimmer primmer skimmer
simmer slimmer swimmer trimmer

IMP
blimp gimp limp pimp shrimp skimp wimp

IMPLE
dimple pimple simple

IN
aspirin been begin bin chagrin chin discipline
feminine fin genuine gin grin harlequin heroine
in inn kin mandolin mannequin masculine
moccasin origin pin saccharine shin sin skin
spin thin tin twin violin win within
also see : "shun", "tion", "ain", "ean", "een"

INCE (INSE)
convince hints mints prince rinse since wince

INCH
cinch clinch flinch inch lynch pinch

IND
behind blind find grind hind humankind kind mastermind mind remind signed unkind unwind wind wined

INDLE
dwindle kindle rekindle spindle swindle

INE
align asinine assign benign breadline combine concubine confine consign decline deadline define design dine divine entwine headline incline line malign mine nine outshine pine porcupine recline refine resign shine shrine sign spine stein swine twine underline undermine vine whine wine

INER
cosigner designer diner eyeliner finer liner miner minor refiner shiner signer

ING
anything bring cling cling ding ding-a-ling evening everything fling king ping ring sing sling spring sting string swing thing ting twing wrtiting
also : add "ing" to other verbs such as "singing", "bringing", "talking", etc.

INGE
binge cringe fringe hinge infringe singe

INGLE
intermingle jingle mingle shingle single tingle

INGO
bingo dingo flaming jingo lingo
also see : "owe"

INK
blink brink chink clink drink fink ink kink link
mink pink rink shrink sink slink stink think wink
zinc

INNER
beginner dinner inner sinner skinner spinner
thinner winner

INSE (INCE)
convince hints mints prince rinse since wince

INO
andantino bambino casino Dino keno Reno

INOR
cosigner designer diner eyeliner finer liner
miner minor refiner shiner signer
also see : "er"

INT
flint hint lint mint print splint sprint squint tint

INX
jinks links lynx minks sphinx thinks winks

ION
buyin' cryin' dandelion denyin' dyin' lyin' Ryan tryin
also see : "in"

IOR
exterior inferior superior ulterior

IP
battleship chip clip dip drip equip flip grip gyp hip lip nip quip rip scrip script ship slip snip strip tip trip whip zip

IPE
gripe hype pipe prototype ripe stereotype stripe swipe type wipe

IPER
piper riper sniper striper swiper typer wiper

IPT
crypt chipped dipped equipped manuscript script sipped slipped transcript whipped zipped

IR
adventure after altar amateur anchor banker better blur canker chauffeur concur confer debtor defaulter defer denture deter falter flanker franker fur grafter halter incur indenture infer laughter letter misadventure occur per prefer purr rafter ranker recur sir slur spanker

spur stir sweater tanker thereafter transfer
venture were wetter
also see : "ear", "air", "ure"

IRCH
birch church lurch perch research search
smirch

IRD
absurd bird blackbird curd heard herd
overheard third word
also see : "ure", "urt"

IRE
admire acquire amplifier aspire attire beautifier
briar buyer choir conspire crier cryer desire dire
drier dryer entire esquire expire fire flier friar
higher hire inquire inspire justifier liar magnifier
multiplier mystifier perspire prior prophesier
require retire satisfier sire squire supplier
testifier tire transpire wire

IRED
*for some words listed in "ire" above, add "d" to
end of word*

IRER
direr enquirer hirer higher inquirer inspirer sire
wirer

IRL
curl earl girl hurl pearl swirl twirl whirl

IRM (ERM)

affirm confirm firm germ reaffirm sperm squirm term worm

IRP
blurp burp chirp twerp

IRROR
cheerer clearer dearer hearer jeerer mirror nearer queerer severer sneerer spearer
also see : "er"

IRST
burst cursed first nursed outburst thirst versed worst

IRT (ERT) (URT)
alert avert blurt comfort concert convert curt desert dessert dirt divert exert expert extrovert flirt hurt insert introvert invert pervert shirt skirt squirt subvert yogurt

IRV (URVE)
conserve curve deserve nerve observe preserve reserve serve swerve

IS (IZ)
biz fizz frizz his is quiz tiz whiz

ISH
abolish anguish demolish devilish dish fish foolish gibberish impoverish polish selfish squish swish tallish wish

ISK
asterisk brisk disk frisk risk whisk

ISP
crisp lisp wisp

ISS
abyss alantis alice amiss analysis bliss carcass
catalyst chalice cowardice Chris Dallas dialysis
dismiss emphasis hiss hypothesis Jist kiss
malice mantis miss nemesis palace paralysis
phallus piss prejudice Swiss Swiss-Miss
synthesis this

IST
accompanist analyst anarchist anthropologist
apprenticed archeologist assist biologist
capitalist catalyst coexist communist consist
cyst dentist desist dismissed egoist essayist
evangelist exist exorcist fatalist fist gist hissed
humanist humorist idealist imperialist insist
journalist kissed list lobbyist missed mist
moralist motorist nationalist novelist organist
perfectionist pharmacist phlebotomist pianist
pissed plagiarist psychologist romanticist
satirist socialist specialist strategist terrorist
twist ventriloquist vocalist wrist
also see : "iss"

ISTED
assisted cysted enlisted existed fisted insisted
listed misted persisted resisted subsisted
twisted

ISTER
assister blister magister mister resister sister
twister

also see : "er"

ISTLE
bristle dismissal gristle missal missile sisal
thistle whistle
also see : "el", "ell", "l"

IT
accredit befit bit carrot clit cockpit comet
commit credit cricket diet discredit edit
ejaculate exit faggot ferret fit git grit kit knit hit
idiot immaculate inhibit legit lit merit minute
mitt parrot pit planet prohibit quiet quit riot shit
sit spirit thicket ticket twit unfit unfortunate
wicket with zit
also see : "et"

ITCH (ICH)
bewitch bitch ditch enrich glitch hitch pitch rich
snitch stitch switch twitch which

ITE
alright appetite bite blight bright byte contrite
copyright daylight delight despite dynamite
excite Fahrenheit fight flight fright headlight
height ignite invite kite knight light midnight
might moonlight night outright parasite plight
polite quite recite reunite right satellite sight
site slight spite sunlight tight trite twilight unite
white write

ITTER
bitter counterfeiter critter fitter fritter glitter litter
quitter sitter transmitter twitter
also see : "er"

ITTY
city committee ditty gritty kitty pity pretty witty

IVE

IV
accumulative active affirmative aggressive
alternative apprehensive appreciative
argumentative attentive attractive authoritative
captive combative communicative competitive
comprehensive consecutive conservative
creative decorative defensive definitive
depressive digressive excessive expletive
extensive figurative forgive fugitive generative
give incomprehensive inexpensive informative
inactive incentive innovative intensive intuitive
inventive live lucrative narrative native negative
offensive operative pensive positive
possessive primitive proactive progressive
prohibitive provocative radioactive reactive
regressive relative representative retentive
sensitive siv successive talkative tentative
vindictive

IVVER
deliver giver liver quiver river shiver sliver
also see : "er"

IXXER (ICKSER)
elixir fixer fixture mixer mixture

IZ (IS)
biz fizz frizz his is quiz tiz whiz

IZE (EYES)
advertise advise analyze apologize arise
authorize baptize buys capitalize capsize
characterize comprise compromise criticize
cries demise deputize despise devise dies
disguise dries economize emphasize
enterprise epitomize eulogize excise exercise
exorcize eyes familiarize fantasize fertilize flies
generalize guys hypnotize idealize idolize
immortalize improvise italicize legalize lies
materialize memorize merchandise minimize
neutralize ostracize paralyze patronize
penalize personalize philosophize pies
plagiarize prize rationalize realize recognize
reprise revise rise satirize scandalize scrutinize
size socialize specialize spies sterilize sties
stigmatize subsidize surprise sympathize
terrorize theorize thighs ties tranquilize tries
utilize Van-Nuys verbalize visualize wise

IZED
Add "d" to IZE

IZZARD
blizzard gizzard lizard wizard

IZZEN
arisen prison risen wizen
also see : "in", "en"

IZZLE
chisel drizzle fizzle frizzle grizzle sizzle swizzle
also see : "el"

IZZY
busy dizzy frizzy tizzy

L

L
apparel barrel bridal bridle cattle chattel carol
embattle homicidal idle rattle suicidal tattle tidal

O

OACH
approach broach coach cockroach encroach
poach reproach roach

OAF (OFE)
loaf oaf

OAST (OST)
boast coast foremost furthermost ghost host
most post roast toast whipping-post

OAT (OTE)
afloat antidote bloat boat coat connote denote
dote float footnote gloat goat misquote moat
note oat overcoat promote quote remote
riverboat rote smote throat tote vote wrote

OATH
both growth loath oath overgrowth undergrowth

OB
blob blowjob bob cob fob gob hob job knob lob
mob nob rob slob snob sob swab throb

OBE
disrobe job globe probe robe strobe

OCAL
focal local vocal yokel

OCEAN (OSHUN) (OTION)
commotion emotion locomotion lotion motion
notion ocean potion promotion

OCK
beanstalk boon-dock clock cock cornstalk
crock deadlock dock flock frock gawk gridlock
hawk hock jock knock livestock lock mock
Mohawk padlock peacock rock shock sidewalk
smock sock squawk stalk stock talk tomahawk
unlock walk wok

OCKET
docket hocket locket pocket rocket socket
sprocket
also see : " it", "et"

ODD (AUD)
abroad applaud awed broad clod cod defraud
façade fraud God nod odd pod prod
promenade quad rod shod sod squad trod wad

ODDY (AUDY)
embody bawdy body gaudy lawdy nobody
shoddy somebody toddy

ODE
ala-mode abode bode code corrode episode erode explode forebode goad load lode mode mowed ode overload rode sowed toad unload

ODDEL
coddle model remodel swaddle toddle twaddle waddle
also see : "el", "ell"

ODGE
dislodge dodge lodge

OF
above dove glove love of shove

OFE (OAF)
loaf oaf

OFF
cough off scoff trough

OFT
aloft loft oft soft

OG
analogue bog catalogue clog cog demagogue dialogue dog epilogue flog fog frog grog hog jog log monologue synagogue

OICE
choice invoice rejoice voice

OID
asteroid alkaloid avoid overjoyed tabloid toyed void

OIL
boil broil coil foil loyal oil recoil royal spoil toil turmoil

OIN
coin groin join loin sirloin tenderloin

OINT
anoint appoint counterpoint disappoint disjoint joint

OISE (OYS)
noise poise

OIST
hoist joist moist rejoiced voiced

OKE
artichoke awoke bloke broke choke cloak coke croak evoke folk invoke joke oak poke provoke revoke smoke soak spoke stoke stroke toke woke yoke

OKER
broker choker mediocre joker poker provoker revoker smoker stoker stroker woke her

OKES
chokes coax folks hoax jokes polks pokes smokes spokes yokes

OLD
behold blindfold bold centerfold cold fold
foothold foretold gold hold household marigold
mold old retold scold sold told uphold withhold

OLE
bole bowl buttonhole cajole casserole coal
control dole droll enroll goal hole loophole mole
oriole parole patrol pole poll role roll scroll soul
stole tadpole toll troll whole

OLLAR
bawler brawler caller collar crawler hauler
mauler scrawler smaller squalor taller

OLLY
collie dolly finale folly golly jolly melancholy
tamale trolley volley

OLT
bolt colt dolt jolt revolt thunderbolt

OLVE
absolve devolve dissolve evolve revolve solve

OMB (ALM)
aplomb bomb calm embalm mom palm psalm
qualm

OMA
aroma coma diploma Oklahoma sarcoma

OMMA (AMA)
comma drama llama mama melodrama pajama

OME
chrome chromosome comb dome foam gnome home honeycomb metronome poem roam Rome tome

OME (UM)
album aquarium auditorium autumn become bottom bum burdensome come cranium crematorium crumb curriculum drum dumb emporium glum gum gymnasium hum kettledrum kingdom martyrdom maximum medium millennium minimum mum museum numb opium overcome pendulum petroleum platinum plum rum sanitarium scum slum some strum succumb sum tedium thumb uranium worrisome yum

OMP
comp pomp romp stomp swamp tromp

ON (AWN)
amazon autobahn bonbon Bonn brawn chiffon dawn drawn echelon fawn gone lawn neon on pawn pentagon silicon swan undergone upon wan yawn

OND
beyond blond bond correspond dawned fond pond respond spawned wand yawned

ONE (UN) (DONE)
anyone begun bun comparison engine everyone fun gun jettison none nun oblivion one outdone outrun overdone overrun

phenomenon pun run shun simpleton skeleton
son stun sun ton undone unison venison

ONER
boner condoner donor groaner honer loaner
loner moaner owner toner

ONG
along belong bong ding-dong gong long ping-
pong song strong thong tong Wong wrong

ONNIC
catatonic chronic diatonic enharmonic
harmonic ironic monophonic philharmonic
phonic platonic polyphonic sonic symphonic
tonic

ONY
alimony acrimony baloney bony crony
macaroni matrimony patrimony phony pony
sanctimony stony testimony

OO (EW)
accrue adieu ado anew avenue bamboo
barbecue bayou blew blue boo brew caribou
cashew chew choo-choo clue construe coo
coup crew cue curfew debut dew drew due
ensue ewe few flew flue glue grew guru
honeydew igloo impromptu interview into issue
Jew kangaroo kazoo lieu misconstrue moo
new outdo overdue pew preview pursue
rendezvous renew residue revenue review
screw shampoo shoe shrew slew slue spew
stew subdue sue taboo tattoo threw through

tissue to too true two undo undue view voodoo withdrew you zoo

OOB (UBE)
boob cube rube tube

OOCH
hooch pooch mooch smooch

OOD
brotherhood could fatherhood firewood good Hollywood hood likelihood livelihood misunderstood motherhood neighborhood should sisterhood stood understood withstood wood would

OODE (UDE)
allude altitude aptitude attitude brood clued conclude crude cued delude dude exclude feud food fortitude gratitude Jude include interlude intrude latitude lewd longitude magnitude misconstrued mood multitude nude platitude preclude prelude pursued prude renewed rude shrewd skewed solitude stewed subdued sued tude wooed you'd

OOF
aloof bulletproof goof hoof proof roof spoof waterproof weatherproof

OOK (UK)
book brook cook crook hook look mistook nook outlook rook shook took undertook

OOKE
fluke kook spook

OOL (UL)
awful beautiful bible bull cool do-able drool dull
dutiful fool full ghoul gull hull jewel Kool lull mull
null pool pull rule school skull spool stool tool
tribal wool
also see : "el", "l"

OOM (UME)
assume bloom boom broom cloakroom
consume costume doom entomb exhume
flume gloom groom loom presume resume
room tomb whom womb zoom

OON
afternoon attune baboon balloon bassoon boon
buffoon cartoon cocoon commune coon croon
dune goon harpoon honey immune
inopportune June lagoon lampoon loon maroon
monsoon moon noon platoon prune raccoon
ruin saloon soon spoon swoon tycoon typhoon

OOP
coop droop dupe group hoop loop nincompoop
poop scoop sloop soup stoop swoop troop
troupe whoop

OOPER (UPER)
cooper hooper looper snooper stupor super

OOR
ambassador ashore auditor bachelor Baltimore
before boar bore chancellor chore commodore

competitor conspirator contributor core corps
corridor deplore dinosaur door drawer editor
emperor encore evermore explore exterior floor
folklore for fore four furthermore galore
governor ignore implore inferior lore lure
matador metaphor more nevermore oar
offshore or orator ore poor pour rapport restore
roar score seashore senator senior shore
snore soar sophomore sore spore store swore
thereafter tore underscore uproar visitor whore
your
also see : "or"

OOSE
caboose goose loose moose noose papoose
recluse spruce truce vamoose Zeus

OOST
boost roost

OOT
afoot foot lead-foot put

OOTE (UTE)
absolute acute astute attribute boot brute chute
commute compute constitute coot destitute
dilute dispute disrepute dissolute electrocute
enroute execute flute fruit hoot loot lute minute
moot mute newt parachute persecute pollute
prosecute prostitute pursuit recruit refute
repute resolute root route scoot shoot snoot
substitute suit toot transmute uproot

OOTH
booth couth sleuth tooth truth youth

OOVE
approve behoove disapprove disprove groove improve move prove remove

OOVER
Hoover groover louver maneuver mover prover remover Vancouver

OOVEY
groovy movie

OOZ
blues booze bruise choose cruise Jews news ooze snooze whose
also see : "use"

OOZER
accuser amuser boozer bruiser cruiser loser muser oozer refuser snoozer user

OP
chop cop crop drop flop hop lollipop mop plop pop prop raindrop shop stop swap tippy-top whop

OPE
antelope cantaloupe cope dope elope envelope grope gyroscope hope horoscope kaleidoscope microscope mope pope rope scope slope soap stethoscope telescope

OPPER
behopper bopper chopper copper cropper dropper eavesdropper eyedropper

grasshopper hopper improper pauper popper
sharecropper shopper stopper swapper
teenybopper topper whopper
also see : " er"

OPT
adopt copped flopped mopped opt popped
stopped

OR
actor behavior benefactor contractor detractor
distracter extractor factor misbehavior packer
reactor refractor sacker savior score slacker
smacked-her tractor your
also see : "oor"

ORA
aura angora flora sinora

ORAL
aural choral floral immoral moral laurel oral

ORCH
porch scorch torch

ORD
aboard accord afford award board bored ford
harpsichord hoard lord overboard poured
reward shuffleboard soared sword ward

ORDER
boarder border disorder hoarder order recorder

ORGAN
gorgon organ Morgan

ORK
cork dork fork New-York pork quirk stork torque uncork

ORM
chloroform conform deform form inform norm perform rainstorm reform snowstorm storm swarm transform uniform warm

ORN
acorn adorn airborne born corn horn morn mourn popcorn scorn stillborn sworn unicorn warn worn

ORROW
borrow sorrow tomorrow

ORSE
coarse course divorce enforce force horse reinforce remorse resource source

ORT
abort assort cavort cavort comfort contort court deport distort escort exhort export extort fort import passport port quart report resort retort short snort sport support thwart tort transport wart

ORTH
forth fourth north

ORTION
abortion contortion distortion extortion portion proportion

also see : "shun"

<u>ORY</u>
accusatory category dormitory dory glory gory
hunky-dory laboratory obligatory observatory
oratory quarry reformatory retaliatory story
territory

<u>OSE</u>
adios close comatose diagnose dose engross
grandiose gross morose nose overdose
varicose verbose

<u>OSE (OZE)</u>
arose chose close clothes compose
decompose depose disclose dispose doze
enclose expose foreclose froze goes hose
impose indispose interpose knows nose owes
pose predispose prose recompose rose
suppose those toes transpose woes
also add "s" to "owe" words

<u>OSH</u>
awash frosh galosh gosh hogwash josh posh
quash slosh squash swash wasa

<u>OSHUN (OTION) (OCEAN)</u>
commotion emotion locomotion lotion motion
notion ocean potion promotion

<u>OSS</u>
across albatross boss cross double-cross floss
gloss loss moss rhinoceros sauce toss

<u>OSSED (OST)</u>

bossed cost crossed exhaust flossed frost
holocaust lost tossed

OST (OAST)
boast coast foremost furthermost ghost host
most post roast toast whipping-post

OST (OSSED)
bossed cost crossed exhaust flossed frost
holocaust lost tossed

OT (OUGHT)
apricot astronaut blot bought brought Camelot
caught clot cot cybot cosmonaut dot forgot
fought gavotte got hotshot jot knot lot naught
not ought plot pot robot rot shot slingshot slot
sought spot squat swat taught thought tot trot
watt what wrought yacht

OTCH
blotch botch crotch debauch notch scotch
watch wristwatch

OTE (OAT)
afloat antidote bloat boat coat connote denote
dote float footnote gloat goat misquote moat
note oat overcoat promote quote remote
riverboat rote smote throat tote vote wrote

OTH
broth cloth froth moth swath wroth

OTHER
another brother mother other smother

OTION (OSHUN) (OCEAN)
commotion emotion locomotion lotion motion notion ocean potion promotion

OTO
koto photo rot Toto

OTTER
blotter daughter hotter otter plotter slaughter spotter squatter trotter water

OTTIC
chaotic erotic exotic hypnotic idiotic narcotic neurotic

OTTO
blotto grotto legato motto staccato

OUCH
couch crouch grouch ouch pouch slouch vouch

OUD
allowed aloud bowed cloud crowd enshroud loud plowed proud shroud

OUGHT (OT)
apricot astronaut blot bought brought Camelot caught clot cot cybot cosmonaut dot forgot fought gavotte got hotshot jot knot lot naught not ought plot pot robot rot shot slingshot slot sought spot squat swat taught thought tot trot watt what wrought yacht

OUNCE
accounts amounts announce bounce counts
denounce dismounts mounts ounce pounce
pronounce renounce trounce

OUND
abound around astound background
battleground bloodhound bound compound
confound downed dumbfound found ground
hound impound mound pound profound
renowned round sound spellbound surround
underground wound
also see : "own (brown)"

OUNG
among clung dung flung high-strung hung lung
rung slung sprung strung stung sung tongue
unstrung unsung wrung

OUNT
account amount count dismount fount mount
paramount

OUR (OWER)
cower devour empower flour flower hour our
plower power scour shower tower

OURNAL (ERNEL)
colonel eternal external fraternal infernal
journal kernel maternal nocturnal paternal

OURNEY (EARNY)
attorney journey tourney

OUS (US)

amorous adventurous ambiguous androgynous
anonymous barbarous blasphemous
boisterous buss cancerous chivalrous
clamorous conspicuous contemptuous
continuous courteous curious cuss dangerous
delirious devious dubious discuss discus
envious erroneous extraneous famous
frivolous furious fuss generous glamorous
gregarious glorious gratuitous harmonious
hazardous hideous hilarious illustrious
incredulous industrious infamous ludicrous
luxurious marvelous miscellaneous
monogamous monotonous muss murderous
mysterious nauseous nautilus nebulous
notorious numerous oblivious octopus ominous
omnibus perilous plus poisonous ponderous
populous posthumous precarious preposterous
presumptuous promiscuous prosperous puss
rebellious rigorous scandalous scrumptious
sensuous serious simultaneous slanderous
spontaneous stimulus strenuous studious
stupendous tedious thunderous thus torturous
tumultuous victorious
also see : "ust"

OUSE
blouse douse grouse house louse madhouse
mouse outhouse penthouse souse spouse

OUT
account about bout clout devout doubt drought
flout gout lout out pout roundabout route
sauerkraut scout shout spout sprout stout tout
boy-scout blow-out wash-out

OVE
clove cove dove drove grove rove

OVE (OF)
above dove glove love of shove

OVER
clover Dover drover moreover over rover

OVER (UVVER)
cover discover hover lover recover rediscover
shover undercover
also see : "her"

OW
allow avow bough bow brow chow cow
disavow endow frau how now plough plow row
slough somehow sow thou vow wow

OWE
afro although arrow banjo barrow beau below
bestow borrow bow bozo buffalo bungalow
calico cargo crow depot doe domino dough
embargo embryo escrow Eskimo flow foe forgo
fro gazebo gigolo glow go grow harrow ho-ho
hoe incognito indigo know largo low marrow
Mexico mistletoe mow narrow no oh outgrow
overflow owe pistachio plateau quo rainbow
ratio roe row sew slow snow so sorrow
sparrow status-quo stow studio tarot though
throw tiptoe to tow tremolo undergo undertow
vertigo woe yo-yo

OWER (OUR)
cower devour empower flour flower hour our plower power scour shower tower

OWING
blowing bowing crowing flowing glowing going growing hoeing knowing mowing owing rowing sewing showing slowing snowing sowing stowing throwing
also see : "ing"

OWL
cowl foul fowl growl howl jowl owl prowl scowl

OWN
alone atone backbone baritone blown bone chaperone clone condone cone cornerstone cyclone Dictaphone flown grindstone groan grown headstone known loan lone microphone milestone moan monotone mown overgrown overthrown own phone postpone prone saxophone sewn shown stone telephone thrown tone trombone unknown xylophone zone

OWN (BROWN)
brown clown crown down downtown drown frown gown noun renown town uptown
also see : "ound"

OX
box chickenpox equinox fox mailbox orthodox ox paradox socks stocks rocks

OY

ahoy annoy boy buoy convoy corduroy coy
decoy destroy employ enjoy Illinois joy ploy soy
toy troy viceroy

OYS (OISE)

noise poise

OZ (AWS)

applause because cause Claus clause claws
gauze gnaws jaws laws menopause Oz pause
paws straws vas was

OZE (OSE)

arose chose close clothes compose
decompose depose disclose dispose doze
enclose expose foreclose froze goes hose
impose indispose interpose knows nose owes
pose predispose prose recompose rose
suppose those toes transpose woes
also add "s" to "owe" words

S

SHUN (TION)

absolution absorption abstention abstraction
acquisition action addiction addition admission
affection affliction aggression ambition
ammunition apprehension ascension attraction
attribution attrition audition benediction
bisection coalition collection commission
competition complexion composition
comprehension compression conception
contraception concession condescension
condition connection constitution contribution

contradiction conviction correction crucifixion
deception definition defection deflection
demolition depiction deposition depression
detection diction digression direction discretion
disposition dissension distribution detention
dimension distraction dissection edition
ejection election electrician electrocution
emission erection eviction evolution exception
execution exhibition expedition exposition
expression extension extraction extradition
faction fiction fission friction fraction ignition
imperfection imposition impression inception
indiscretion infection inhibition inquisition
inspection institution intention intermission
intersection intervention intuition introspection
invention jurisdiction magician mathematician
mention mission musician nutrition objection
obsession omission opposition oppression
partition perception perfection permission
petition physician politician pollution position
possession preconception prediction
prosecution profession progression prohibition
projection proposition prostitution protection
reaction reception recession recognition
reflection regression rejection rendition
repetition repression requisition resolution
resurrection restriction retention retribution
retrospection satisfaction secession section
selection solution statistician substitution
succession submission subtraction superstition
suppression suspension technician tension
traction tradition transaction transgression
transmission transposition transition tuition
also see : "in"

T

TION (SHUN)
absolution absorption abstention abstraction
acquisition action addiction addition admission
affection affliction aggression ambition
ammunition apprehension ascension attraction
attribution attrition audition benediction
bisection coalition collection commission
competition complexion composition
comprehension compression conception
contraception concession condescension
condition connection constitution contribution
contradiction conviction correction crucifixion
deception definition defection deflection
demolition depiction deposition depression
detection diction digression direction discretion
disposition dissension distribution detention
dimension distraction dissection edition
ejection election electrician electrocution
emission erection eviction evolution exception
execution exhibition expedition exposition
expression extension extraction extradition
faction fiction fission friction fraction ignition
imperfection imposition impression inception
indiscretion infection inhibition inquisition
inspection institution intention intermission
intersection intervention intuition introspection
invention jurisdiction magician mathematician
mention mission musician nutrition objection
obsession omission opposition oppression
partition perception perfection permission
petition physician politician pollution position
possession preconception prediction
prosecution profession progression prohibition

projection proposition prostitution protection
reaction reception recession recognition
reflection regression rejection rendition
repetition repression requisition resolution
resurrection restriction retention retribution
retrospection satisfaction secession section
selection solution statistician substitution
succession submission subtraction superstition
suppression suspension technician tension
traction tradition transaction transgression
transmission transposition transition tuition
also see : "in"

U

U (EW) (OO)

accrue adieu ado anew avenue bamboo
barbecue bayou blew blue boo brew caribou
cashew chew choo-choo clue construe coo
coup crew cue curfew debut dew drew due
ensue ewe few flew flue glue grew guru
honeydew igloo impromtu interview into issue
Jew kangaroo kazoo lieu misconstrue moo
new outdo overdue pew preview pursue
rendezvous renew residue revenue review
screw shampoo shoe shrew slew slue spew
stew subdue sue taboo tattoo threw through
tissue to too true two undo undue view voodoo
withdrew you zoo

UAL

actual contractual dual duel factual manual

UB
bub club cub grub hub hub-a-bub pub rub
scrub shrub snub stub sub tub

UBE (OOB)
boob cube rube tube

UBBLE
bubble double rubble stubble trouble

UCK
amuck buck chuck cluck deduct duck fuck luck
muck pluck potluck puck struck suck truck tuck
also see :"uct"

UCKER
bucker chucker clucker fucker pucker
seersucker sucker trucker

UCT
abduct conduct construct deduct instruct
obstruct plucked viaduct
also see :"uck"

UD
blood bud cud dud flood mud scud spud stud
thud

UDE (OODE)
allude altitude aptitude attitude brood clued
conclude crude cued delude dude exclude feud
food fortitude gratitude Jude include interlude
intrude latitude lewd longitude magnitude
misconstrued mood multitude nude platitude
preclude prelude pursued prude renewed rude

shrewd skewed solitude stewed subdued sued
tude wooed you'd

UDDER
butter rudder shudder udder
see also : "utter"

UDDLE
cuddle fuddle huddle muddle puddle
also see: "el"

UEL
cruel duel fuel jewel

UDGE
budge drudge fudge grudge judge misjudge
nudge smudge

UFF
bluff buff cuff duff enough fluff gruff huff muff
scuff snuff stuff tough

UFFLE
duffle muffle ruffle scuffle shuffle truffle
see also : "el"

UG
bug drug dug jug hug mug plug pug rug shrug
slug smug snug thug tug

UGE
centrifuge huge Scrooge stooge

UGGLE
buggle juggle smuggle snuggle struggle

UILT (ILT)
built guilt hilt jilt kilt quilt spilt stilt tilt wilt

UK (OOK)
book brook cook crook hook look mistook nook
outlook rook shook took undertook

UKE
duke juke puke uke

UL (OOL)
awful beautiful bull cool do-able drool dull
dutiful fool full ghoul gull hull jewel Kool lull mull
null pool pull rule school spool stool tool wool
also see : "el", "l"

ULCH
gulch mulch

ULGE
bulge divulge indulge

ULK
bulk hulk sulk

ULSE
convulse impulse pulse repulse

ULT
adult catapult consult cult difficult exult insult
occult result

UM (OME)
album aquarium auditorium autumn become
bottom bum burdensome come cranium
crematorium crumb curriculum drum dumb
emporium glum gum gymnasium hum
kettledrum kingdom martyrdom maximum
medium millennium minimum mum museum
numb opium overcome pendulum petroleum
platinum plum rum sanitarium scum slum some
strum succumb sum tedium thumb uranium
worrisome yum

UMBER
cucumber cumber encumber lumber number
slumber umber

UMBLE
bumble crumble fumble grumble humble
jumble mumble rumble stumble tumble

UME (OOM)
assume bloom boom broom cloakroom
consume costume doom entomb exhume
flume gloom groom loom presume resume
room tomb whom womb zoom

UMP
bump chump clump dump hump jump lump
plump rump slump stump thump trump ump

UN (DONE) (ONE)
anyone begun bun comparison engine
everyone fun gun jettison none nun oblivion
one outdone outrun overdone overrun

phenomenon pun run shun simpleton skeleton
son stun sun ton undone unison venison

UNCH
brunch bunch crunch hunch lunch munch
punch scrunch

UND
cummerbund fund refund rotund shunned

UNE (OON)
attune commune dune immune inopportune
tine
afternoon attune baboon balloon bassoon boon
buffoon cartoon cocoon commune coon croon
dune goon harpoon honey immune
inopportune June lagoon lampoon loon maroon
monsoon moon noon platoon prune raccoon
ruin saloon soon spoon swoon tycoon typhoon

UNDER
blunder plunder thunder under wonder

UNG (OUNG)
among clung dung flung high-strung hung lung
rung slung sprung strung stung sung swung
tongue unstrung unsung wrung young

UNGE
lunge plunge sponge

UNK
bunk chunk drunk dunk flunk funk hunk junk
monk plunk punk shrunk skunk slunk spunk
stunk sunk trunk

UNNY
bunny funny honey sunny

UNT
affront blunt brunt bunt confront cunt forefront
grunt hunt punt runt shunt stunt

UP
cup buttercup pup sup up

UPER (OOPER)
cooper hooper looper snooper stupor super

UPPER
cupper supper upper

UPT
abrupt corrupt cupped disrupt erupt interrupt
supped tupped

URB
blurb curb disturb herb perturb suburb superb
verb

URCH
birch church lurch perch research search
smirch

URD (ERD)(IRD)
absurd bird curd herd heard third turd word

URDER
girder herder murder

URE
adventure allure amateur anchor assure
banker blur brochure caricature chauffer
concur confer cure defer demure denture
endure ensure expenditure flanker franker
forfeiture immature impure indenture insecure
insure liqueur literature lure manicure mature
miniature misadventure obscure overture
pedicure premature pure ranker reassure
secure signature slur spanker stir sure
tablature tanker temperature your venture
also see : "err", "air", "ear", "or"

URGE (ERGE)
converge dirge diverge emerge merge purge
sourge serge splurge submerge surge urge
verge

URING
alluring assuring blurring concurring conferring
curing deferring demurring deterring during
enduring ensuring incurring inferring insuring
interring luring maturing referring securing
spurring transferring whirring
also see : "ing"

URN (EARN)
adjourn burn churn concern discern earn fern
intern kern learn overturn return sojourn spurn
stern taciturn turn urn yearn

URNT (ERNT)
burnt weren't

URSE (EARSE)

adverse converse curse disburse disperse
diverse hearse immerse inverse nurse purse
rehearse reverse terse transverse traverse
universe verse worse

URST (ERST)
burst cursed first nursed outburst worst

URT (ERT)
alert avert blurt concert convert curt desert
dessert dirt divert exert expert extrovert flirt
hurt insert introvert invert pervert shirt skirt
squirt subvert yogurt

URVE (IRV)
conserve curve deserve nerve observe
preserve reserve serve swerve

URY (ERRY) (EARY) (AIRY)
adversary airy arbitrary beneficiary berry bury
canary capillary cautionary cherry commentary
culinary customary dairy dictionary dietary
dignitary disciplinary discretionary evolutionary
extraordinary fairy ferry hairy hereditary
honorary imaginary intermediary legendary
mercenary military momentary monetary
mortuary nary necessary obituary ordinary
planetary prairie pulmonary reactionary
revolutionary sanctuary sanitary scary
secretary seminary sherry solitary stationary
temporary very visionary vocabulary voluntary
wary

URRY
curry flurry fury hurry jury Missouri scurry slurry surrey worry

US (OUS)
amorous adventurous ambiguous androgynous anonymous barbarous blasphemous boisterous buss cancerous chivalrous clamorous conspicuous contemptuous continuous courteous curious cuss dangerous delirious devious dubious discuss discus envious erroneous extraneous famous frivolous furious fuss generous glamorous gregarious glorious gratuitous harmonious hazardous hideous hilarious illustrious incredulous industrious infamous ludicrous luxurious marvelous miscellaneous monogamous monotonous muss murderous mysterious nauseous nautilus nebulous notorious numerous oblivious octopus ominous omnibus perilous plus poisonous ponderous populous posthumous precarious preposterous presumptuous promiscuous prosperous puss rebellious rigorous scandalous scrumptious sensuous serious simultaneous slanderous spontaneous stimulus strenuous studious stupendous tedious thunderous thus torturous tumultuous victorious
also see : "ust"

USE (Z Sounding)
abuse accuse amuse blues booze choose clues confuse cruise cues diffuse dues fuse infuse Jews lose misuse muse news peruse

pews re-use refuse shoes snooze sues stews twos use views zoos

USE (S Sounding)
abuse deduce duce excuse induce introduce juice misuse obtuse produce profuse reduce reproduce seduce Syracuse

USH
blush brush crush flush gush lush mush plush rush slush thrush underbrush

USH
bush cush push

USK
dusk husk musk tusk

UST
adjust August bust crust disgust distrust encrust entrust gust just lust mistrust must robust rust thrust trust unjust

USTLE
bustle corpuscle hustle muscle mussel rustle tussle

UT
but butt cut glut gut hut mutt nut putt rut shut slut smut strut uncut

UTCH
clutch crutch Dutch hutch much retouch such touch

UTE (OOT)
absolute acute astute attribute boot brute chute commute compute constitute coot destitute dilute dispute disrepute dissolute electrocute enroute execute flute fruit hoot loot lute minute moot mute newt parachute persecute pollute prosecute prostitute pursuit recruit refute repute resolute root route scoot shoot snoot substitute suit toot transmute uproot

UTER
commuter computer cuter muter neuter persecutor polluter prosecutor suitor tutor

UTTER
butter clutter cutter flutter gutter mutter putter shutter sputter strutter utter
also see : "udder"

UVVER (OVER)
cover discover hover lover recover rediscover shover undercover
also see : "her"

UZ
abuzz because buzz cause does fuzz was

X

X (EX) (ECKS)
complex decks duplex ex flex necks pecks reflex rolodex sex specs unisex

THE END

KASEYEMM

Wyoming Valley, Pennsylvania